CONTENTS

ON THE MENU

Grizzly bears are built to live and hunt in harsh, cold places. The bears have powerful bodies and thick fur. They live in parts of Canada and the north-west United States.

Grizzly bears are **omnivores**. They hunt **prey** such as deer, moose and fish. They also eat berries, insects and dead animals.

FACT

Outside of Alaska, there are only about 1,000 grizzlies left in the United States. Humans have used up much of the land where the bears once lived. Because of this, fewer grizzlies are born each year.

omnivore animal that eats plants and other animals

prey animal hunted by another animal for food

GRIZZLY BEARS
— BUILT FOR THE HUNT —

by Lori Polydoros

Consultant: Dr. Jackie Gai, DVM
Wildlife Vet

Raintree is an imprint of Capstone Global Library Limited, a company incorporated in England and Wales having its registered office at 7 Pilgrim Street, London, EC4V 6LB – Registered company number: 6695582

www.raintree.co.uk
myorders@raintree.co.uk

Editorial Credits
Brenda Haugen, editor; Juliette Peters, designer; Tracy Cummins, media researcher; Katy LaVigne, production specialist

Printed in China.

ISBN 978 1 474 70200 3
19 18 17 16 15
10 9 8 7 6 5 4 3 2 1

British Library Cataloguing in Publication Data
A full catalogue record for this book is available from the British Library.

Photo Credits
Getty Images: Barrett Hedges, 19, Don Johnston, 17; Minden Pictures: Michio Hoshino, 1, 15; Shutterstock: AndreAnita, 11, Galyna Andrushko, 12, Gleb Tarro, 8, 13, Greg and Jan Ritchie, 14, Jeffrey B. Banke, 3, Jim David, 2, 10, Nagel Photography, Cover, pashabo, Design Element, riekephotos, 6, saraporn, 7, Scott E Read, Cover Back, 5, 9; SuperStock: Animals Animals, 21.

Every effort has been made to contact copyright holders of material reproduced in this book. Any omissions will be rectified in subsequent printings if notice is given to the publisher.

All the internet addresses (URLs) given in this book were valid at the time of going to press. However, due to the dynamic nature of the internet, some addresses may have changed, or sites may have changed or ceased to exist since publication. While the author and publisher regret any inconvenience this may cause readers, no responsibility for any such changes can be accepted by either the author or the publisher.

EXPERT SNIFFERS

Grizzly bears are deadly **predators** with a keen sense of smell. They bow their heads low and sniff as they walk. Grizzlies sniff for prey and other food. They can smell an animal **carcass** from about 3 kilometres (2 miles) away.

FACT

A grizzly's sense of smell is seven times better than a bloodhound's. Police in some parts of the world use these dogs to track the **scent** of criminals.

predator animal that hunts other animals for food

carcass body of a dead animal

scent smell of something

LOOK AND LISTEN

Grizzlies have good vision. They see about as well as humans do. But grizzly bears see even better at night. They often stand on their back legs to look for prey.

Grizzlies hear twice as well as humans do. They also hear in every direction. A young grizzly bear's round ears grow to full size before the rest of its body. Grizzlies can hear prey in a thick forest.

FACT

A grizzly's ear has a balloon-shaped bone that makes sounds louder.

DANGEROUSLY FAST

With strong upper bodies, grizzlies can power across land. A big shoulder hump made of muscle makes a grizzly fast and strong. A grizzly can chase prey at speeds of 56 kilometres (35 miles) per hour. With their strength, grizzlies can easily overpower their prey.

FACT

Grizzlies can be 3 metres (10 feet) tall when standing on their back legs. They can weigh up to 544 kilograms (1,200 pounds).

A FISHY FEAST

Fish is the main source of food for grizzlies living in the north-west United States. Grizzlies are powerful swimmers. They swim in rivers full of salmon. The salmon swim upstream to lay eggs. Grizzlies catch the fish in their mouths! The bears can eat more than 45 kilograms (100 pounds) of salmon a day.

DIGGERS

Grizzly bears have sharp claws that grow to about 10 centimetres (4 inches) long. They use their claws to grip prey. They also dig up plants and rip open logs. These diggers can destroy **burrows** to reach squirrels or mice. Their powerful legs and paws can break bones in one swipe.

FACT

Grizzlies also use their paws to move rocks. They uncover moths hiding there. A grizzly can eat 20,000 moths a day!

burrow tunnel or hole in the ground made or used by an animal

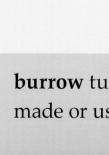
14

GRIND IT UP

A grizzly bear can bite hard enough to crush a bowling ball or bite through a cast-iron frying pan. It uses its 42 strong, sharp teeth to tear and grind food.

A grizzly bear has a huge mouth that can open up almost as wide as a 30-centimetre (12-inch) ruler.

FACT

Grizzlies have deadly **canine** teeth. These teeth work like scissors to shred meat.

canine long, pointed tooth

SURPRISE ATTACK!

A grizzly bear sometimes **ambushes** its prey. It may **stalk** a group of North American elk. The bear will attack with a burst of speed. The grizzly will aim for a young elk trailing behind the herd. The bear will use its fierce paws to knock down the animal. The grizzly bear will kill its prey quickly.

ambush attack by surprise
stalk hunt an animal in a secret, quiet way

WHAT'S THAT SMELL?

Grizzlies smell, but for a good reason. The bears rub their bodies over dead animals to hide their own smell. Then they can sneak around without their prey knowing they are near. This makes the bears even more dangerous to their prey!

AMAZING BUT TRUE!

Grizzly bears **hibernate** for up to seven months each year. To get ready for hibernation, the bears eat extra food and double their body fat. They do not eat, drink or go to the toilet during hibernation. Their heartbeats slow from 40 beats per minute to just 8 beats per minute.

hibernate spend winter in a deep sleep

A grizzly bear hibernates in a den.

GLOSSARY

ambush attack by surprise

burrow tunnel or hole in the ground made or used by an animal

canine long, pointed tooth

carcass body of a dead animal

hibernate spend winter in a deep sleep

omnivore animal that eats plants and other animals

predator animal that hunts other animals for food

prey animal hunted by another animal for food

scent smell of something

stalk hunt an animal in a secret, quiet way

READ MORE

Mammals (Animal Classification), Angela Royston (Raintree, 2015)

Omnivores (What Animals Eat), James Benefield (Raintree, 2015)

River Food Chains (Food Chains and Webs), Angela Royston (Raintree, 2014)

WEBSITES

www.bbc.co.uk/nature/life/Bear

Learn more about all types of bear.

www.nps.gov/yell/learn/nature/gbear.htm

Learn more about the grizzly bears that live in Yellowstone National Park, USA.

COMPREHENSION QUESTIONS

1. How do grizzly bears use their senses to hunt?

2. What makes grizzly bears well suited to living and hunting in cold weather?

INDEX